Also by Glen Baxter

THE
IMPENDING
GLEAM

THE
IMPENDING
GLEAM

Glen Baxter

Alfred A. Knopf New York 1982

Library of Congress Cataloging in Publication Data
Baxter, Glen.
The impending gleam.

1.   English wit and humor, Pictorial.
I. Title.
NC1479.B29A4 1982   741.5'942   81-48126
ISBN 0-394-52473-X   AACR2

To Bill and Phyllis

CONTENTS

THE
IMPENDING
GLEAM

WAY
OUT
WEST

PECOS BILL HAD A "THING"
ABOUT HOUSEHOLD DUST.....

"I PRUNE MY CHRYSANTHEMUMS THIS-A-WAY...."

JEDSON WAS NOTED FOR HIS WITHERING
SIDELONG GLANCES

"THE WAY 1 FIGGER 1T — TRUTH <u>1S</u>
UN-TRUTH 1NSOFAR AS THERE
BELONGS TO 1T THE RESERVOIR OF
THE NOT-YET-REVEALED, THE
UN-UNCOVERED 1N THE SENSE OF
CONCEALMENT" REASONED McTAGGART

YOUNG HANK ENTERTAINED THE BOYS
WITH A FINE DISPLAY OF SMOULDERING

"I KEEP MY BAGELS IN HERE"
WHISPERED THE DESPERADO

AT THE GIVEN SIGNAL, MRS BOTHAM
POPPED OUT FROM THE CONCEALED
LINING AND BLASTED THE RATTLER

BIG JEB WAS A TRICKY CUSTOMER
ALL RIGHT

IT WAS TOM'S FIRST BRUSH
WITH MODERNISM

Professions of the Old West

No. 2

The Dentist

WILD BILL WAS KNOWN TO GO TO EXTRA-
ORDINARY LENGTHS TO CATCH "THE LUCY
SHOW" REPEATS ON CHANNEL SIX

VANCE LIVED IN CONSTANT FEAR
OF LOSING HIS WRISTWATCH....

"I STUB MY CIGARS OUT........ THERE!"
SNORTED THE TEXAN

"BUT SURELY, LANGUAGE IS NOT
DEFINED FOR US AS AN ARRANGE-
MENT FULFILLING A DEFINITE
PURPOSE...." STAMMERED JED

FRUITS OF THE WORLD
IN
DANGER

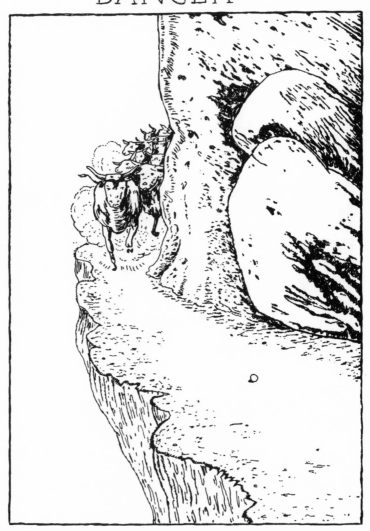

Number 10   The Apricot

IT WAS THE HALITOSIS KID.....

"I'VE CALLED ABOUT THE POST OF ASSISTANT
MILLINER" DRAWLED DEKE

YOUNG ERIC HAD PREPARED HIMSELF FOR
ALMOST ANY EMERGENCY....

PANCHO'S SLEEPING ARRANGEMENTS WERE
THE TALK OF THE BUNKHOUSE

" SO YOU SEE, BOYS — WHAT A PICTURE MUST
HAVE IN COMMON WITH REALITY, IN ORDER
TO BE ABLE TO DEPICT IT — CORRECTLY OR
INCORRECTLY — IN THE WAY IT DOES, IS
ITS PICTORIAL FORM" EXPLAINED TEX

SETH TOOK HIS TEA AT SEVEN ON THE DOT

"I MAKE A LIVING PEDDLING
DANDRUFF" SNORTED THE
OLD TIMER

McGUIRE SEEMED TO HAVE RIDDEN
INTO A TRAP......

THE LOMAX BOYS KEPT UP AN ALL-NIGHT
VIGIL ON THE NOUGAT

HE WAS FORCED TO ENDURE TERRIBLE
IMPERSONATIONS OF ANNETTE FUNICELLO

"TO ME THE WINDOW IS STILL A
SYMBOLICALLY LOADED MOTIF"
DRAWLED CODY

HOW HE HATED SATURDAY
MORNING SHOPPING

GREAT
MOMENTS
IN HISTORY
Number 43
The First Omelette

IT WAS A MONDAY AFTERNOON JUST LIKE
ANY OTHER.....

From the Pages
of History

IT WAS A SMALL VOTIVE BUST OF
CONNIE FRANCIS.....

ROBIN WAS CERTAINLY IMPRESSED WITH
THE SIMULATED TEAK FINISH

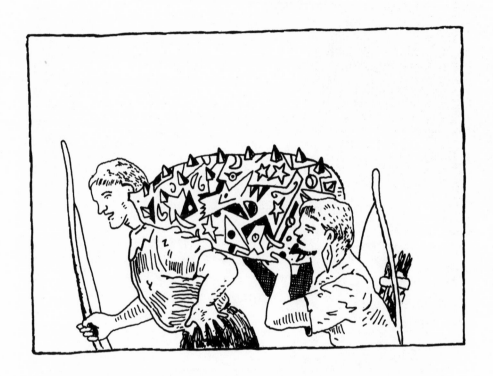

YOUNG ARTHUR'S EARRINGS WERE
THE TALK OF NOTTINGHAM

IT WAS THE SMALLEST PIZZA THEY HAD
EVER SEEN

"NOT SO FAST, VARLET — I DEMAND A SECOND
FITTING!" BELLOWED SIR PEREGRINE

FRUITS OF THE WORLD
IN
DANGER

Number 12 The Kumquat

SIR ROLAND TRIED TO CONVINCE THE
SCEPTICS OF THE POTENTIAL OF HIS
LIGHTWEIGHT "MINI-SHIELD".......

IT WAS HUNGARIAN COOKING ALL RIGHT

"WHAT HAVE YOU DONE WITH MY
WIMPLE?" GROWLED BIG 'BULL' HARPER

GREAT FAILURES
OF OUR TIME

№ 16

The First Yo-Yo

THE TWO MEN WERE IN AGREEMENT
—IT WAS A WORK OF SOME MERIT

THE TWO MEN WERE IN AGREEMENT
— IT WAS A WORK WITHOUT MERIT

IT WAS HORRIBLE. FROM MY VANTAGE POINT
I COULD SEE THE STRUGGLING FIGURES
BEING CARTED INTO PROFESSOR TREMBO'S
STRUCTURALIST FILM SEMINAR

"AH YES, MR. WRIGGLESWORTH — IT'S ABOUT
THIS.....AHEM.....FIRST DRAFT OF YOUR
NOVEL" SPLUTTERED MR. SCELPE

HE TOOK HER IN HIS ARMS AND
GENTLY SQUEEZED HER GOATEE

FRUITS OF THE WORLD
IN
DANGER

Number 1   The Orange

BERYL HAD HIT UPON A WAY
OF RELIEVING THE TEDIUM OF
MISS ABERGHAST'S LESSONS

"I SENSED THAT BRENDA WAS TRYING
TO IMPRESS ME....."

IT HAD BEEN SUSPECTED FOR SOME TIME
THAT MAVIS WAS EXPERIMENTING WITH
A COMBINATION OF BALKAN AND
TURKISH BLENDS

DAPHNE BEGAN TO SENSE SHE WAS NO
LONGER ALONE.....

ANGELA ADDRESSED THE
MEMBERS OF THE CROCHET
CLUB ON HER PROPOSALS FOR
DEALING WITH LATECOMERS

"GOING DOWN TO THE VILLAGE
AGAIN, EH?" SNAPPED MADGE

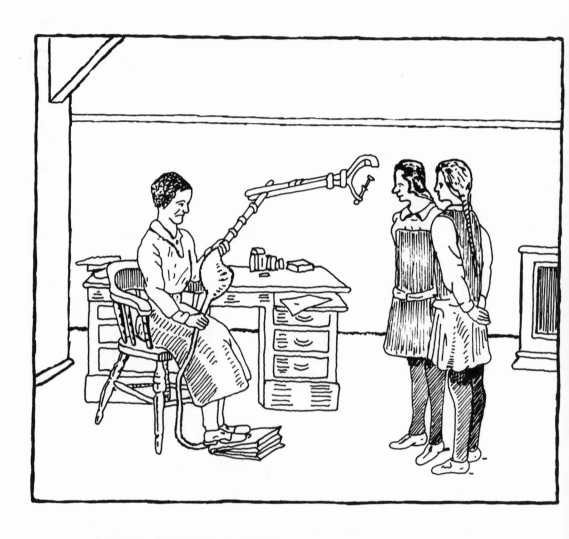

MISS FROBISHER MADE A POINT OF
THREATENING NEW ARRIVALS
WITH "THE NOSE TWEAKER"

DEIDRE POINTED OUT HER SUPPLY OF HASHISH
FOR THE AUTUMN TERM

AFTER TEA, MONICA WAS FORCED TO
ENACT THE GRIM RITUAL OF
"COUNTING THE STUMPS"

MIRANDA HAD STUMBLED UPON OUR
SUPPLY OF BEARDS.......

"SO YOU'RE THE MYOPIC MULDONI BOYS
FROM CHICAGO, EH?" SPAT LANNIGAN

"I SUPPOSE YOU'RE ALL WONDERING WHY
I'VE GATHERED YOU HERE TODAY"
WHISPERED THE BOSUN

GREAT FAILURES
OF OUR TIME

№ 160 The First Pencil Sharpener

HE WAS NOT THE MAN SHE HAD
LOVED THAT EVENING IN
BRIDGEPORT......

GUSTAV'S NEON WIMPLE WAS CLEARLY
FAILING TO IMPRESS THELMA

"SOME ARE HAM AND SOME ARE CHEESE
AND PICKLE" CONFIDED PANDOWSKI

HE WAS FROM BROOKLYN ALL RIGHT

GERARD INSISTED ON FLAUNTING HIS
REVOLUTIONARY THERMAL SNOOD

THE MANAGER WAS STRONGLY
RECOMMENDING THE SCROD

IT WAS THE FOURTH TIME THAT DADDY HAD
FALLEN FOR THE EXPLODING FORK ROUTINE......

THERE WAS A HINT OF TRIUMPH IN
UNCLE FRANK'S BLUE EYES

THERE WAS GENUINE CONCERN IN
DAPHNE'S FRANK BLUE EYES

THE NURSE ENTERED WITH THE
BRIGADIER'S CALORIE—CONTROLLED
BREAKFAST.....

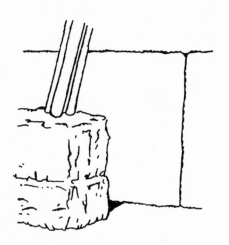

The SHADOW OVER DRINGFIELD

"I HOPE YOU CAN EXPLAIN THAT
MOUND OF PEANUT HUSKS IN MY
BEDROOM!" SNAPPED GATTING

WITH AN AIR OF WEARIED RESIGNATION
PROFESSOR COOMBES TUCKED THE ESSAY
BACK INTO MY BEARD

"WHEN THIS IS SWITCHED ON, YOUR PANTS
WILL BE CLEANED AND PRESSED EVERY
TWO MINUTES" SNAPPED TOWLE

THE LADS HAD A WAY OF DEALING
WITH BORING OLD RELATIVES

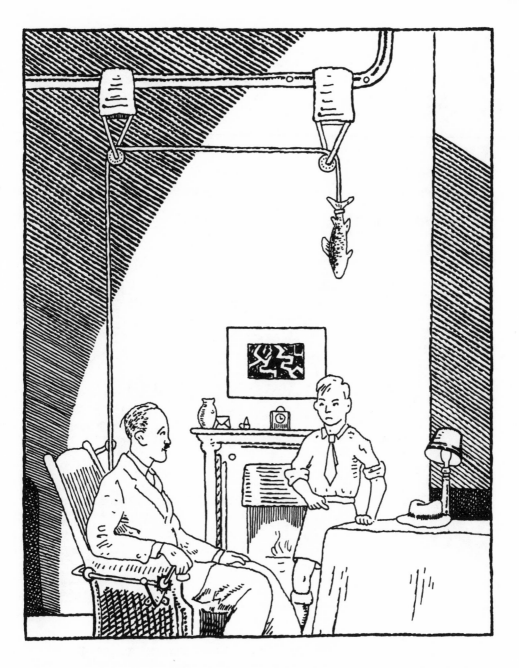

AS THE AFTERNOON WORE ON I BEGAN TO
SUSPECT THAT MR PHELPORT WAS INDEED
KEEPING SOMETHING FROM ME

YOUNG TALBOT STOOD UP AND WITH A
SHRIEK OF TRIUMPH WHISKED OFF HIS
BOATER TO REVEAL THE FORBIDDEN
POMPADOUR......

THERE WAS STILL MUCH TO
LEARN ABOUT SZECHUAN
CUISINE

"THERE'S ONLY ONE WAY TO
EAT WHELKS" HISSED GREIG

"IF THERE HAS BEEN A MISHAP ON THE SPORTS
FIELD THEN NATURALLY I WANT TO BE THE
FIRST TO KNOW" MUMBLED THE HEADMASTER

SUNDAYS CAME AROUND WITH
DEPRESSING REGULARITY

"I'M AFRAID IT'S GRIM NEWS,
SANDY— THE VICE-CONSUL
INTENDS TO BAN THE
WEARING OF WIMPLES
AFTER 7:15 P.M"

IT WAS A DEVICE FOR TURNING SCHOOL MEALS
BACK INTO FOOD

HE HAD BEEN CAUGHT USING THE
FORBIDDEN "HEAD PEN" AGAIN.......

BARTWELL SAW THROUGH THE DISGUISE
ALMOST IMMEDIATELY

"NOW WHICH ONE OF YOU IS MRS. BLOYARD?"
ASKED THE INSPECTOR

HAMMOND OUTLINED THE RUDIMENTS
OF HIS DARING ESCAPE PLAN

"BUT......I...ORDERED THE
CHICKEN KIEV..." BLURTED COOPER

"I'LL THANK YOU TO STOP JUGGLING MY
GHERKINS!" SNORTED THE ANGUISHED THROGUE

ESSENTIAL SUPPLIES WERE
DROPPED TO THE BRITISH
AGENTS

A NOTE ABOUT THE AUTHOR

During the last ten years Glen Baxter has exhibited his drawings and paintings in New York, Amsterdam, and London. His work has also appeared in numerous small publications and magazines. *The Works*, a collection of his prose and drawings, was published in New York in 1977; *Atlas* appeared in Amsterdam in 1979.

Glen Baxter lives in London and is currently working
on a revolutionary new process to
vulcanize the wimple.

A NOTE ON THE PRODUCTION OF THIS BOOK

The text of this book was hand lettered by the author, who also hand drew all of the display type in imitation of the typeface Caslon Antique. To conform with his design, the small amount of copy appearing in type was set in Caslon Antique.

Printed and bound by American Book–Stratford Press, Saddle Brook, New Jersey

Designed by Sara Reynolds